"*The Exit Process* is a solid f[...] departments. Loaded with practical and insightful information, tools, and resources on everything related to an employee's departure. An easy-to-read (and use) book for HR departments of any size. The authors walk you through every possible scenario. Highly relevant and useful for all HR practitioners."

—**Paul Boyles**, SPHR, SHRM-SCP,
Executive Coaching LLC

"The beginning of an employee's journey is discussed frequently in business—interviewing, hiring, and onboarding—and Amanda and Brenda provide an improved process and tools for each topic in *The Team Solution Series*. Yet, how to prepare for an employee's last day is often overlooked. *The Exit Process* is an excellent guide to the end of the employee journey. This book rounds out the series, providing easy-to-implement tools for all businesses to remain professional upon an employee exit while protecting your team and company."

--**Stephanie Collins**, Internship & Equity Coordinator,
Maryville College Career Center

"With higher turnover in the job market these days, a roadmap is needed that benefits both the company and person in transition. *The Exit Process* is the book every HR department needs in their hands. All angles are covered with the goal of creating a win/win for everyone involved. Brenda and Amanda have placed integrity and grace at the forefront of what many times is an awkward situation."

—**Bill McConnell**, Author and Project Lead
of the Conquer Yourself Project

"As a solopreneur, I appreciate the practicalities outlined in *The Exit Process*. Even if your team, like mine, is composed exclusively of 1099 contractors, you need a plan for releasing them. Regardless of the reason for the exit, having the right processes in place will ensure your business doesn't miss a beat. A quick but thorough overview, *The Exit Process* equips you to protect your business and prepare the way for smooth transitions."

—**Erin K. Casey**, author and owner,
My Writers' Connection

"Such insightful information! As a business owner, the art of learning how to not burn bridges is an essential facet of your success story. We want as many referrals as possible when marketing our businesses, and what a fabulous referral an ex-employee can be in the long run. I applaud Brenda and Amanda for bringing solid solutions to the table for human resources."

—**Lisa Veatch**, Ad Agency Owner & Business
Development Professional

THE EXIT PROCESS

HOW TO
PROFESSIONALLY PART WAYS

Other Books by the Authors

The Team Solution Series

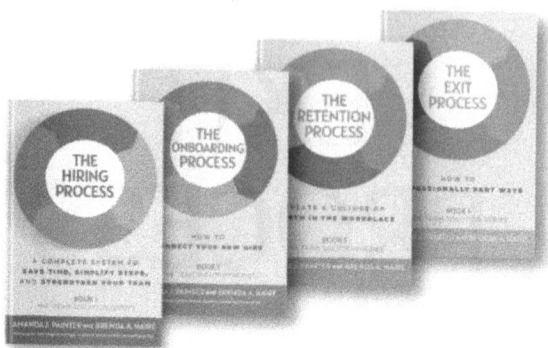

The Author Solution Series

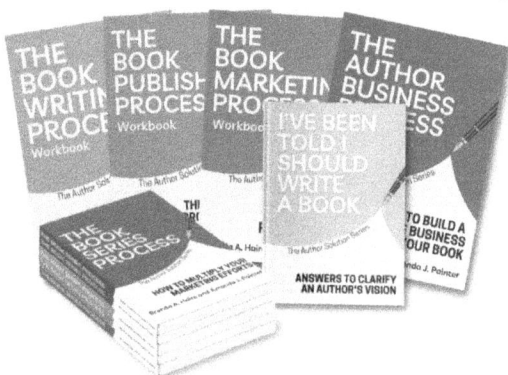

Also by Brenda A. Haire

TheJoyOfPursuit.com

THE EXIT PROCESS

HOW TO
PROFESSIONALLY PART WAYS

AMANDA J. PAINTER
and
BRENDA A. HAIRE

BOOK 4
THE TEAM SOLUTION SERIES

Joy of PURSUIT PUBLISHING

Throughout the book, you'll be introduced to new tools. We provide examples, templates, checklists, worksheets, and more.

Download your free bundle at
TheJoyofPursuit.com/Exit

@JoyofPursuit

Dedication

We dedicate this book to those brave enough to move on when necessary, those who create cultures no one wants to leave, and those left behind after someone exits. Our hope is that your leadership implements this series and honors your value and grace-given gifts.

Contents

Foreword

As a diversified entrepreneur for almost twenty years, I've exited companies and have experienced employees exiting my businesses. I understand first-hand the value shared here in The Exit Process. As you will read, protecting your business assets and company culture should be a priority for all business owners.

Sadly, most small businesses don't invest in Human Resources. Entrepreneurs and small business owners hire on the fly, and since many are visionaries, they are focused on their next big vision and don't pay enough attention to those exiting their companies. This leaves them open to potential losses—assets, other employees following suit, clients, revenue—the list is endless. Preparation is the key to protection.

I'm often quoted as saying,

> "What's OBVIOUS to you is MAGIC to other people."

This is the gold Brenda and Amanda share: The obvious process for company exits. What makes it magic is that most business owners haven't given it much thought, but these authors map out the process complete with the tools needed for implementation.

If you are serious about growing a sustainable business, this book and series is a must-read but also must be implemented. Whether you have an HR manager or you're handling these responsibilities, managing the human side of your business is vital. You invest time, energy, and resources, and the goal of business is to multiply them, not waste them. Understanding what is at stake and how to prepare for the various exits, including your own, will help you become a company that no one wants to leave. When you take the necessary steps to implement a proper exit strategy, your team, clients, and colleagues will take notice.

In the fast-paced social media environment, you better understand how quickly your company can become vulnerable if an employee exit isn't handled properly. Oddly enough, this isn't covered in most branding courses or business-building courses. You'll learn about your target audience, what products and services to offer, maybe your business structure, but very little if anything is covered concerning the human resources it takes to run and maintain a healthy business.

Regardless of the size of your business, your team matters and how you handle any exits that arise says more about you and your company than most business owners realize. Congratulations on taking the right steps to prepare for the inevitable.

—**Dr. Brian J. Dixon**, best-selling author of *Start with Your People: The Daily Decision that Changes Everything*, news producer and host of the Social Media Marketing Talk Show

A Note to You—the Reader

Professional is not a label
you give yourself; it's a description
you hope others will apply to you.

—David Maister

No one considers endings when starting a company or hiring an employee, but all good things eventually come to an end. Seasons change, people change—turnover is inevitable. Acknowledging this and anticipating the needs is the solution to the unavoidable exit. You can't predict the unexpected, but you can have a plan in place to respond to circumstances that are out of your control.

Business owners often find themselves incredibly dependent on their staff, especially in small businesses. For a company with a staff of twenty, one employee is 5 percent of the workforce. That leaves a significant impact when one exits.

What happens when an employee leaves is often overlooked. It is unlikely that you have a process in place—it's something you hope you won't need, so it is pushed to the back burner. Employees exiting your company can be abrupt and disruptive, but planning ahead will allow for a smooth transition.

Being prepared for the exit of any of your company's employees or contractors will prevent a loss in productivity and an unnecessary culture shift. As in the other books in *The Team Solution Series*, communication is an ongoing theme here too. We teach you how to prepare for the worst while keeping the rest of your team in the loop and onboard.

Prepare for exits with a proper system in place and a solid onboarding and retention process. If you know your employees are cross-trained well, as we recommend in *The Retention Process*, and you have a clear list of assets, as we teach in *The Onboarding Process*, the transition during and after an exit will be less destructive to your company as a whole.

Finish the exiting employee's journey professionally and with the same intention as it started. This type of consistency speaks to your culture of worth. Even if someone leaves under less-than-ideal circumstances, a structured exit process will send them off with a positive experience with your company. Ideally, it will be streamlined and stress-free.

We will cover different types of exits and how to plan accordingly. We include what challenges to look out for, how to communicate with your team to preserve culture, the proper way to transition any role, and how to evaluate the situation to avoid continual turnover in the future, if possible.

Having a process in place *before* your employee tells you they're leaving is key. Take the time to ensure it is effective and efficient. This will include revisiting departments and checklists you created in *The Onboarding Process*. Of course, now your goals will be slightly different.

Like all books in *The Team Solution Series,* we've provided a Toolbox to assist you with your exit process. If you haven't yet, download it now to follow along, as we discuss the tools throughout the book. Let's get started.

Chapter One

Preparation and Protection

Plan for what is difficult while it is easy.

—Sun Tzu

While we often hear how important first impressions are, final impressions are no less valuable. How you say goodbye will likely be what people remember most.

The two main goals in *The Exit Process* are preparation and protection. We will set you up to achieve success in both.

Preparation

If you've been with us through this entire series thus far, congratulations—you are ahead of the pack when it comes to preparing for an employee exit. The three previous books, which cover employee hiring, onboarding, and retention, set you up with the right tools and procedures to handle the final employee process—the exit.

The first practical way to prepare for anyone in the company leaving is to have Standard Operating Procedures (SOPs) documented for key tasks within all positions.

When an employee leaves, it is not the right time to ask them to document SOPs for their role. Their heart probably resigned long before they told you they were leaving, so why would they at this point want to put forth the effort?

What the employee does, as well as when and how they accomplish it, should be in the SOP. If you don't currently have SOPs, it's time for your team to create them. SOPs are necessary tools that set up consistent, repeatable, streamlined processes for how tasks are done. *The Team Solution Series* could be considered SOPs for your Human Resources Department, as the books provide clear processes for HR practices. Each book includes the checklists and tools required for building and leading a successful team.

Some SOPs can be lengthy and elaborate. Don't be intimated by this thought. Start small and work through the basic steps. Here is an example of a simple SOP.

Sample SOP

Name: Blog Publishing SOP

Purpose:
Ensure posting of high-quality blog content and related graphics that meet company specifications and branding guidelines.

Procedure steps:
- Writer composes a blog post based on the predetermined topic from the company content calendar.
- Writer sends the draft to the copy editor for review.
- Copy editor makes changes and sends them back to the writer for review/approval of changes.
- Writer shares blog topic with graphic designer for blog images.
- Graphic designer creates images with blog title for website and social sharing and shares with writer.
- Writer sends the final blog and graphics to the Content Manager.
- Content Manager does final proofread of blog post.
- Content Manager posts to website and on social media accounts.

Resources:
- Sample blog post
- Editing guidelines
- Branding Guide
- Social media calendar and passwords

SOPs are also useful for cross-training. All positions should be cross-trained and/or have a support person standing by to fill in when needed. SOPs allow for ease of cross-training and help employees who may not perform a particular function regularly recall the important procedural steps. In *The Retention Process,* we said, "Cross-training can expedite growth." Yes, it can expedite growth when everyone is happy and on board, and it can prevent growth from coming to a halt upon someone's exit.

If you are a small business, cross-training your employees is especially needed to stay productive if someone exits. You can't afford to wait for the replacement hire to get up to speed if the day-to-day responsibilities of that role affect your output. If you only have one person responding to customer service emails, and that person quits, who will handle their inbox? Cross-train someone whose role interacts with the same processes and/or people. The training time will be shorter and more productive. Every position in your organization should be cross-trained, or at the very least backed up by another employee. Find your backups now, and you'll be one step closer to adequate preparation.

SOPs and cross-training are the two practices that should be in place long before someone announces their departure. Work with your Leadership Team and HR Department to organize your SOPs. Then create a Cross-Training Organization, Accountability, Responsibility Chart (CT OAR). This chart uses the same boxes as the OAR Chart explained in *The Retention Process*, but it includes the person or people who can support or back up each role in the case of an absence, including vacations, sick days, or departures.

Below, you will see an example of an OAR Chart followed by a CT OAR Chart for the same department.

Customer Service Department OAR Chart

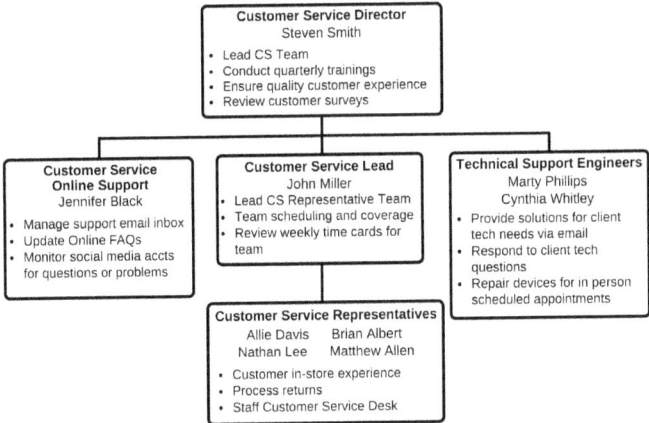

Customer Service Director
Steven Smith

- Lead CS Team
- Conduct quarterly trainings
- Ensure quality customer experience
- Review customer surveys

Customer Service Online Support
Jennifer Black

- Manage support email inbox
- Update Online FAQs
- Monitor social media accts for questions or problems

Customer Service Lead
John Miller

- Lead CS Representative Team
- Team scheduling and coverage
- Review weekly time cards for team

Technical Support Engineers
Marty Phillips
Cynthia Whitley

- Provide solutions for client tech needs via email
- Respond to client tech questions
- Repair devices for in person scheduled appointments

Customer Service Representatives
Allie Davis   Brian Albert
Nathan Lee   Matthew Allen

- Customer in-store experience
- Process returns
- Staff Customer Service Desk

Customer Service Department Cross-Training OAR Chart

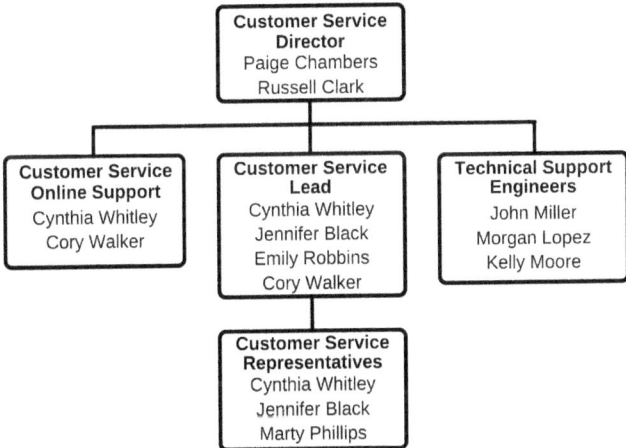

Customer Service Director
Paige Chambers
Russell Clark

Customer Service Online Support
Cynthia Whitley
Cory Walker

Customer Service Lead
Cynthia Whitley
Jennifer Black
Emily Robbins
Cory Walker

Technical Support Engineers
John Miller
Morgan Lopez
Kelly Moore

Customer Service Representatives
Cynthia Whitley
Jennifer Black
Marty Phillips

Protection

How a company treats its people, especially on their way out, speaks volumes. Protecting four key areas in your company may be the determining factor when others consider working *for* you or *with* you. Your team, and likely your clients, will notice when someone has left your company. How they view the departure greatly depends on your response.

A professional exit process will protect your:

1. Company culture
2. Assets
3. Relational currency
4. Reputation in the marketplace

Company Culture

You've heard it before: "One bad apple can spoil the whole bunch." It is true. Be certain *you* are not the bad apple. When someone leaves, how you treat them and how you communicate with the rest of the company will protect your culture. If you have a culture worth protecting, the employee could be leaving for a variety of reasons that may not be negative. Don't create chaos or drama where there isn't any.

As we unfold the exit process, you'll discover ways to protect your culture. Remember, when people leave, others will notice, and they will care more if it directly impacts their day-to-day workflow/load. Implementing this process will help avoid disruptions to the greatest extent possible.

If your team can temporarily handle the additional workload upon an employee's exit, be sure to discuss the parameters and ensure them that you are diligently working to fill the position. If the role requires additional responsibilities that merit temporary additional pay, discuss that as well. Rewarding employees who pick up the slack is often overlooked in companies, and that can be detrimental to your culture in the long run. When adding additional responsibilities to a team member, keep in mind that goals and deadlines already in place may need adjusting. Revisit Goal MAPs (See Toolbox), if applicable, adjust as needed to accommodate for these new responsibilities.

Assets

Protect your assets—your company property, current employees, and bottom line. Any time an employee leaves, your security risk increases. Introduce the proper measures to protect your data and finances and mitigate security risks.

This exit process will also provide ways to keep productivity high while transitioning employees. Be aware that one employee's exit could lead to more following suit, consequently protecting your revenue stream during any transition is important.

You'll need resources to either restructure or rehire.

Proper offboarding can assist your company in avoiding legal issues, **Protect your revenue stream during transition.** such as wrongful termination lawsuits, compensation disputes, or contract violations. All of which are costly and time-consuming. Document the process as you work through it, review contracts made with the employee, and always consult a legal professional when necessary to mitigate any misunderstandings. Having a process with a paper trail will promote clarity and keep everyone "on the same page."

Relational Currency

Not all employees leave forever—especially if you have a healthy company culture. They may realize the grass isn't greener on the other side and miss what they had with you. It may be that whatever circumstances caused them to leave change, and they are available to return at a future date.

We've seen employees leave when a change in their marital status moved them farther from the office than they were willing to commute. Later, when commuting was no longer an issue, we welcomed that employee back.

When it comes to relational currency, whether you want the employee to return or not, remember that they are likely friends with some of your current employees and/or clients. Don't disregard someone because they choose not to work at your company.

Employees can also turn into customers. They know your products and services better than anyone. If they leave on good terms, they may be future customers and potential referral partners.

Reputation in the Marketplace

Reputation matters. Never miss an opportunity to obtain feedback, especially from an employee who is on their way out the door. Feedback is an opportunity for learning and growth. Allowing the exiting employee to share the good, the bad, and the ugly with you is better than them sharing the bad and the ugly in the marketplace. Remember not to take it personally and understand there is no reason to attempt to change their mind. Listen and gather feedback. (We will guide you through gathering and examining the feedback and turning it into opportunities for your company in Chapter 6.)

Having a seamless transition is important internally as well as externally. Don't stop producing or serving your clients because an employee leaves. The wheels must stay in motion. Clients need a smooth transition too, especially if the employee worked directly with them in a project management role, for example. Never blame the employee or criticize them to the client. Transition the client to a more experienced employee or possibly someone in leadership to avoid repeating the cycle. Ensure the client feels valued and isn't neglected during the transition.

Applying the above strategies will assist you and your company with preparation and protection.

Chapter Two

Types of Exits

*Good employees quit
when management is bad.
Bad employees quit
when management is good.*

—Peter Drucker

There are a variety of ways (and reasons) that employees leave. Here we'll cover the typical exits and how to respond appropriately. Each has unique challenges.

The predominant type of employment in the United States is considered "at will." This means that an employer can terminate an employee at any time and for any reason (apart from illegal hiring/firing practices, such as discrimination). And it works the same for the employee; they can quit, with or without cause or advance notice.

As covered in *The Onboarding Process*, employment legalities must be followed at both the federal and state level. These laws vary from state to state and are ever-changing. You must invest time and resources for your business to be compliant—no exceptions. Consult an attorney to be sure you understand all that is legally required to be an employer. It pays to follow the rules, laws, and regulations upfront. If you are in the United States, you can view more details about Equal Opportunity Employment and discrimination here: eeoc.gov. Outside the U.S., please check with your governing authorities.

Resignation

When an employee resigns, it should be in writing. If an employee verbally resigns, ask them to provide a brief letter. This should note the day they submit their resignation and their last date of work. Your employee is not obligated to tell you why they are leaving or where they are going to work next if they have secured a new job.

The resignation letter should be submitted to your HR Department or the team member who fulfills this role. (If your team is small, it may be someone on your Leadership Team or the company owner.) HR will then handle notifying the appropriate team members and initiating the exit process.

If your employee shares their reason for leaving, listen. Don't make assumptions. Also, inform your employee that they will have more opportunities to share using the Exit

ScoreCARD and during the Exit Interview (more on these in Chapter 6).

Resignation can be perceived as rejection, especially if you are a small company and haven't encountered it much. It's important to keep your emotions in check. It's normal to feel abandoned, hurt, or disappointed. You may be emotionally attached to the time, money, or other resources that were poured into this person. Now, you have to start all over again with a new hire. This can be one of the most challenging parts of owning a business.

It's human nature to want to avoid rejection or attempt to change the person's mind. Which brings up the question: Is there ever a time to convince an employee to stay?

Occasionally, it may be worth it but not often. Before asking a resigned employee to stay and attempting negotiations with them, talk with your Leadership Team and take it through the appropriate HR channels. Examine why you want them to stay. Is it because you're avoiding the feeling of rejection? Do you feel you've wasted resources on them? Or is it because they are a stellar employee?

Also, if a reason for leaving is shared, examine it. Is it in your control? Or is it a different issue? Know that mental resignation happens long before the act of resigning. For an unhappy employee, the actual resignation is the final act of a loss of hope. If an employee is leaving because they feel unappreciated, you can't try to appreciate them on their way out. It's too little, too late.

Money motivates to a point, and people rarely leave solely because of it. If you convince them to stay for more money or more vacation time, it is likely a BAND-AID© on the surface of a deeper problem.

Mental resignation happens long before the act of resigning.

Be aware that if you convince an employee to stay, it can often backfire on you and create more issues.

Once, in an organization that had not dealt with much resignation before, a team member submitted her resignation letter directly to the owner of the company. The company was small and working to implement structure, but overall, it was lacking. The owner made a knee-jerk reaction and immediately called the team member and asked her to stay. He did this without fully reading her resignation letter or consulting anyone on his Leadership Team about the employee or her performance. He didn't work directly with the employee and had no context for how she was fulfilling her role.

He was able to convince the team member to withdraw her resignation and stay on the team. After that conversation, he contacted his Leadership Team to inform them of the situation. He quickly discovered that he should have let her go. This employee had been resisting the structure that her supervisor was establishing. The employee was difficult to work with—abrupt and rude to other team members. Her exit would have been a welcomed relief for many on the team.

Upon fully reading her resignation letter, the team discovered her venting about other employees, frustration with structure, avoiding accountability, and other behaviors that highlighted why she was not the right fit for the company.

This situation caused turmoil in the company, frustration among the Leadership Team, and a host of other issues. Eventually, the problem employee resigned *again*. This resignation was taken without trying to win her back. But much of this chaos could have been avoided if the first resignation had been accepted and a better fit found for the position sooner.

Employees who resign will land anywhere on the spectrum regarding employee performance. The two extremes are when you're happy an employee is leaving or devastated at the thought of losing them. Let's examine a few items specific to each of these situations.

When a Resignation Is a Relief

There will be those employees who you are happy to see go. For whatever reason, they were not the right fit with your team, your culture, or the role. This could be for a variety of reasons—not meeting Core Values, poor performance, et cetera. While it is a relief that this employee decided on their own to leave and you didn't have to fire them, be sure to examine why you want them gone. Identify why they aren't a fit and don't repeat the same mistake when replacing them.

When you set standards and expectations and hold your team accountable to them, it will often cause those who aren't suitable to leave on their own. This may be the nudge a problem employee needs to resign.

When Your Best Resigns

Unfortunately, the opposite will also happen: your star team member or top performer will decide it's time to move on. These situations are more challenging. They can be disappointing and even scary. This is when emotions can take a toll—anger, sadness, worry, regret, and so on. Take a deep breath and stay calm managing your emotions. This is not the time to place guilt on the one leaving or to upset the rest of the team.

While you may experience frustration, disappointment, or even betrayal, slow down enough to show the employee your gratitude—not only for their work but for them as a person.

We know you may heavily rely on this person. Your mind immediately goes to "how will

I survive without them?" You will, and this process will help.

This situation, as with any departure, requires attention and action. But it is unnecessary to map out your entire plan during the initial conversation. Take time with your Leadership Team to discuss the transition, especially if there were any stipulations in the resignation.

Specific Stipulations of a Resignation

Depending on the situation or employee's position, their resignation may have specific stipulations attached to it. These typically regard tasks or responsibilities they will or won't own during their transition time.

Examine their stipulations closely and discuss with all the necessary parties. Request clarification from the exiting employee, if needed. Only agree to stipulations you can follow through on without disrupting the team or exit process.

After agreeing to any stipulations, be sure you communicate these as needed to your team. This communication is *your* responsibility, not the responsibility of the employee who has resigned. *Lead* your team through this transition. It is unreasonable to expect the exiting employee to lead a team they will no longer be working with.

For example, if your HR Director is leaving, they may stipulate that they will not interview job candidates during their transition time. This needs to be communicated as other departments may be in the middle of hiring. By having the proper cross-training and/or support team members in place, this stipulation will be communicated to the team member who will be taking over this responsibility during the transition.

We've seen department heads with open positions attempt to schedule interviews on the calendar of the exiting HR Director because their exit and stipulation were not properly communicated. This wasted valuable time during the hiring process and showed a lack of concern for the team, culture, and interview candidates. We discuss proper communication more in-depth in Chapter 4. Remember that healthy communication will keep your culture intact and ensure productivity remains steady.

Retirement

A retirement announcement is often the easiest to hear. But it can be difficult to transition, especially if the employee has been with your company for a long time. Relationships can't be replaced. This employee is likely a valuable asset to your team.

Longevity has many benefits. If possible, consider some alternatives to retirement. Would this employee consider moving to part-time? This could be for a specific amount of time or indefinitely. Would they be willing to train a new employee or work on specific projects once in a while?

Another option would be to hire them as a consultant. Is there a particular skill or type of project that this employee enjoys and your company would benefit from their continued input?

Any of these alternatives will lessen the blow and allow for an easier transition—for the company *and* the employee. They can ease into their retirement while still receiving compensation. And it shows that you value their knowledge and skills.

If one of these options is offered/accepted, remember the intention. This type of arrangement should be mutually beneficial. These are not alternatives to avoid replacing the employee. Don't try to keep them doing the same job but in fewer hours. It's devaluing and won't work in the long run.

Whether the employee decides to make a clean break or a slower transition, take the time to celebrate their contributions to the company. This will show the remaining employees that the retiree's efforts were appreciated. Additionally, use the Leave a Legacy Worksheet found in the Toolbox to capture the knowledge that comes with this type of tenure.

Termination

Termination will be the most challenging exit to deal with, which is why having a process in place is essential. Small business owners often find themselves ill-equipped for dealing with termination. Firing is stressful and uncomfortable. It can also have legal consequences if not handled correctly. Let's step through how to handle this delicate situation properly.

Remember your Core Components, especially your Core Values. It is your responsibility to lead your company to perform well and serve your clients. You cannot achieve this if you aren't willing to hold your team accountable to your Core Values and performance standards.

If you have disciplined an employee according to the policy laid out in your Team Handbook and their behavior doesn't change, it is time for *you* to make a change to better your team. When you have to fire someone, always meet in person and in private. If face-to-face isn't an option, at the minimum, handle it verbally over the phone and follow up with a written notice. NEVER fire over email or text.

Your HR representative should handle this conversation if your company is big enough to have an HR Department. If not, it may be the owner or CEO of the company who handles firing. Regardless, never fire alone. Always have someone else in the room (virtually or in-person). These conversations can be emotional, and having someone to witness or mediate is crucial.

Be prepared. Never fire when you are emotional or in the heat of the moment. If this employee has made a critical error, you still need to take a moment, consult with the necessary team members, and create a plan before firing them.

Cover any necessary legal items. This is why your HR Department's involvement is essential. Know what legal compliance is necessary for employee termination.

Firing should never be a surprise. An employee should never be blindsided by being terminated. Supervisors should have regular check-ins and reviews with all employees in your company. In *The Retention Process,* we walk you through Quarterly and Annual Direct Report Meetings in which supervisors and the employee discuss their performance and set goals. Employees should also be held accountable to their goals in regular department meetings. (If you're not discussing metrics in your meetings, you need to start.)

If you're ready to fire **Firing should** someone but have no **never be** documentation of previous **a surprise.** problems, use the Goal MAP to create an improvement plan. This gives them the opportunity to hear your feedback and improve. Then, if appropriate action is not taken, you have documentation that supports your grounds for termination.

When necessary take immediate action with a plan or a termination. Delaying could hurt your entire team. When it's time for someone to go, you *must* let them go. The conversation will likely be difficult, but avoiding it will create more chaos. Keeping problem team members is a disservice to your other employees, your clients, and *even* the problem employee. When you allow them to stay, you're lowering your standards and signaling to other employees that subpar work or not being a team player is acceptable. This behavior can be infectious and incredibly detrimental to your company. Handling a necessary termination in a timely manner also signals to low performers what won't be tolerated.

When scheduling the termination meeting, there should be little time between setting the meeting and the actual meeting. This is best handled swiftly. Be direct and brief. Don't spend the first ten minutes discussing the problems. Go ahead and tell them that they are being terminated. Support your decision by sharing unmet performance goals and/or examples of unshared Core Values. If applicable, reference previous disciplinary actions, highlighting the corrections and feedback that had been given but not followed.

Avoid arguing or entering long discussions. Some may dispute their termination. This isn't the time to debate or allow a lengthy rebuttal. Balance the time by allowing them to share their thoughts while setting the exit in motion.

Provide next steps. Expedite the turning in of assets and restricting access (see Chapter 5 for more details). Gather any information needed to make the transition to their replacement or temporary substitute a smooth one. Are they in the middle of a project? Do they have clients waiting for responses?

Have all necessary paperwork prepared in advance. A simple termination letter should include their last date of work and any compensation plan. Calculate and communicate final compensation, severance pay, or employee termination payments. Ask them to sign the letter during the meeting to confirm their understanding. If they refuse to sign, have it signed by the others present and note that the employee declined.

Lastly, never make promises out of guilt. Only offer references or other connections when warranted. Thank them for their time with your company and wish them well.

Layoffs

While firing someone is often said to be one of the most difficult tasks for a leader, laying someone off is equally challenging. Some may even consider it harder. For many leaders, it feels like they have failed their employee. By laying off, the company leadership admits that they are at fault for no longer having a position for the employee to fill. This could be due to downsizing, lack of sales, a failed product, and other such issues. Admitting fault can be humbling.

Before laying someone off, be absolutely certain that there is no other available position that they qualify for. On the flip side, never create a position for someone in order to dodge emotions.

Prior to a layoff, work with your Leadership Team to begin their Transition Plan, but resist finalizing it until after meeting with the employee. (We will share more on the details of a Transition Plan in Chapter 5). First and foremost, always meet face-to-face, as with firing. When explaining a layoff to an employee, be direct but gentle. Tell them specifically why they are being laid off.

Being vague can cause **Always meet** discord and cause the **face-to-face.** employee to question your real motives. Provide a written statement to the employee with the specifics you discuss in the meeting.

Continue the conversation by expressing your gratitude for the work they have done for your business. Don't expect the employee to immediately be ready to discuss transitions and timelines. While you may have agonized over this decision for a long time, it may have come out of the blue for them. Allow them time to process, even if that includes a bit of time off. (Maybe allow them to leave their shift an hour early or take the afternoon out of the office.) Show compassion and treat them with dignity and respect. Specify a time you'll follow up with them to finalize their Transition Plan.

If possible, assist them with finding a new job. While this isn't your responsibility, if they are a valuable team player and you have a connection, this gesture will express your gratitude for their work and your confidence in their abilities. Write them a glowing letter of recommendation. Connect them with other companies that are hiring. If possible, be flexible with their work schedule to allow them to interview for other positions.

It is naive to think that this employee will still give 100 percent of the effort they did before. Their mind is probably preoccupied with finding a new job. But the more compassionate and helpful you are to them during this time period will also benefit you. If you're empathic while they are processing the disappointing news and they see your effort to help them find a new job, they will be more likely to continue to put forth their best effort.

Also, it is common for employees not to work through their entire transition timeline. This is not personal. If you plan an exit that slowly transitions them out over a six-week time frame, they may find a new job that wants them to start sooner. Be respectful and understanding of this situation, happy they secured new employment, and prepared to carry on without them.

Company Dissolved

For whatever reason, if the decision is made to close the company doors, take special care in handling the exit process for your entire team. The timeline for winding the business down will vary depending on the circumstances and will probably take longer than the typical two weeks' notice.

Respect for your team should be a top priority. While you'll have many tasks on your desk to finalize, it might be best to have your Leadership Team transition the other employees. The components of the previous layoff section should be taken into consideration. Always communicate this type of closure face-to-face. No one wants to hear that they are losing their job, but it's unacceptable for them to find out via email or the rumor mill.

The timeline of dissolving a company may not be definitive or go exactly as planned.

There will be many unknowns throughout the process. Keep everyone up to date on a regular basis. Continuing the communication demonstrates value and respect. Especially keep employees informed about how their final pay will be processed or any changes to other time-tracking procedures.

To avoid your team throwing in the towel, ensure they see that you haven't.

Continue to work hard, show up as a leader, strive to serve your clients well, **Integrity matters.** and follow through on promises made. Be sure to express gratitude for your team's commitment.

Some employees may not stick around until the end. Think through how you will handle this. It may be necessary to hire temp workers to help you finish out your timeline.

Communicate professionally to clients and vendors about the closing, and never neglect the remaining customers or the quality of your product. Sustain the same level of service you have always provided. Integrity matters, even at the end. You may or may not know what your future holds, and some of these employees and/or clients might be included in that future. Preserve relationships with open and honest communication.

Department Transfers

Never overlook offboarding in one department if an employee accepts a position elsewhere in the company. This could include a change in the assets they have access to. Avoid the assumption that established employees know other department's procedures. Use the short checklist below to guide you through the exit process from one department to onboarding in another.

Department Transfer Checklist

☐ Broadcast appropriate announcements company-wide.

Update:
    ☐ OAR Chart
    ☐ CT OAR Chart
    ☐ Website
    ☐ Team Directory

☐ Introduce the transfer to departments and key roles that intersect.

☐ Change access to software, emails, projects, channels, etc.

☐ Notify Accounting of pay increases, if applicable, and when those go into effect.

☐ Provide any training needed for this specific role. All procedures may vary for each department.

☐ Allow time for introductions and opportunities for creating relationships.

☐ Post the open position, if applicable.

☐ Have the transferring employee complete a Leave a Legacy Worksheet, if applicable.

Every situation will be unique and provide its own challenges. Approach all with the same professional manner to ensure you protect your company's assets and team, while valuing the employee who is exiting.

Chapter Three

Challenges

Expect obstacles and face them head-on.
They are going to come up, so the way you
handle them is what makes all the difference.

—Lance Dale

While difficult situations could accompany any employee exit, you may face some uncommon or particularly challenging situations at some point. A challenging employee exit should make you pause and revisit your onboarding, retention, and possibly even your hiring processes. Was this employee ever the right person for your company? Did you overlook the fact that they didn't share your Core Values, but you hoped their skills and performance would compensate for it?

Being aware of potential challenges doesn't mean you can prevent them or they won't arise, but you will be better prepared when they do. Having your entire Leadership Team and department leads read *The Team Solution Series* is a valuable first step in preparing your team. Be sure to discuss all aspects and tools of the series and decide how you will implement the processes and handle the unique challenges that could occur at any stage of the employee journey.

No Notice or Walkout

Ideally, you want to part ways on good terms and with plenty of notice. Hopefully, the employee shares the same desire. The typical protocol would be for an employee to provide two weeks' notice to allow for a smoother transition. This may not always be the case, though. Whether they call it quits after a stressful meeting, leave a note on your desk, send an email stating, "I quit," or simply fail to show up, an abrupt departure is challenging. Having a plan in place that you can immediately initiate will help control the damage.

Utilize your CT OAR Chart to determine backup for the position, ensuring essential work isn't neglected. Depending on the employee's role, consider utilizing a temporary contract worker to assist in the interim. This can help lighten the remaining team's load and allows time to properly fill the position. Desperation never leads to smart hiring decisions. Preparation will prevent desperation, and the best preparation happens when you are not in an emergency situation.

Please Go Ahead and Leave

There may be times when an employee is so toxic to the work environment that you want them to go immediately. They give you a two weeks' notice, but you would rather they leave now. This usually applies to an employee you're already considering firing.

Or you may need an exiting employee to leave sooner than two weeks due to the sensitivity of their job role. Do they have access to critical information? If they are no longer invested in your company, it's best to release them from their role without asking for two weeks or adequate time to find a replacement. More damage could be done in that short time span than is worth it just to keep up appearances or avoid a productivity gap.

If you are about to tell someone not to work out their notice, first consult with the HR or legal professional on your team. You'll need to ensure that a binding contract isn't in place with the employee that states otherwise. Typically, this is not the case but avoid assumptions.

Also, if you allow them to leave early without compensation for this time, some states will view it as a termination as opposed to a resignation. This can trigger the qualification for unemployment, depending on the situation. One option is to continue their compensation for the time period but allow them to discontinue working. This will, of course, need to be stated in writing.

Be cautious about keeping someone around longer than necessary. A generous employee may give a long notice, but you may or may not want to take advantage of it.

When an employee **Damage can be** resigns, move rapidly to **done in a short** transfer their duties to **time span.** someone else. Even those with the best of intentions may not give their best efforts if they know they won't be around long enough to deal with the repercussions of subpar work. Consider if a notice of any length is beneficial to the company and the team overall before accepting it.

Resigns the Wrong Way

All resignations must go to the HR representatives for your company regardless of its size. You need someone to be accountable and up-to-speed on HR processes. Be sure to include clear exit procedures in your Team Handbook for how to resign. (In *The Onboarding Process Toolbox*, we provide an outline of what should be included in your Team Handbook.) Even if the process is in place and clearly stated in the handbook, not all employees will follow it. All team supervisors need to know whom to direct a resignation to, should someone directly turn in their notice to them, and what next steps to take.

The supervisor should direct the employee to HR or suggest they go together if the employee isn't comfortable doing so on their own. HR needs to oversee the exit process because they know the full scope of the employee's benefits, assets, and access points. The HR representative can then work with the supervisor on the Transition Plan and replacement.

When Quitting Is Contagious and Others Jump Ship

When people leave, others may also go. One employee's departure, especially a respected employee or leader, will often cause others in the company to begin questioning their own job satisfaction. The same influence the employee had with the team that once worked in your favor may now work against you. Employees may start exploring other employment options. The odds of this increase when the exiting employee is well-liked and respected.

Exodus typically happens with those who worked closely with the exiting employee—their team members or peers and especially their subordinates. This supervisor may be the primary reason some employees enjoyed working at your company. It's possible that employees in a certain department felt their supervisor protected or buffered them from a harsher leader in the organization. They may feel that when their ally is gone, they will have to deal with the harsh leader themselves.

Another reason employees follow an exiting leader could be because that leader wasn't holding their team accountable to goals, deadlines, or schedules. Aware they had a lax leader, the employees took advantage of the situation. Now, they realize they need to exit, too, before a new leader comes in and expects accountability.

Mass Exodus

If the entire team walks out at once or within a short period of time, you need to evaluate the situation. If multiple employees from multiple departments leave, you need to ask yourself some hard questions. Are you the problem? Are your actions aligned with your Company Core Components (or CCCs; see *The Retention Process*)? If you are saying one thing and doing another, your team will lack inspiration and drive. Are you abusive in meetings or constantly crossing boundaries? Are you neglectful? Is your company Vision changing, but you are not communicating it well? There are many reasons for a mass exodus, but you'll need to search for the common denominator.

Once you identify the root issue, take action to transition the remaining team members to a new Vision, change your leadership style, or rebuild your team to align with the way you conduct business. If your company is outdated and you resist change, you need to hire accordingly. If you are changing directions with your Company Core Components, you will need a plan to transition your clients, or you'll lose them as well.

Handling major shifts in Vision with care and buy-in from your team can help you avoid a mass exodus. People may still leave over time if they realize the new direction isn't for them, but at least you've properly communicated and shown respect to your team by allowing them the necessary time and information to properly process the situation.

Damage Control

A resignation or termination will cause a ripple effect. Some remaining employees may resent picking up the leftover workload.

Others may question why someone is leaving. Whenever dealing with people, remember that emotions are involved. There may be blame, concern, or worry. On the other hand, there may be excitement. The remaining team might now see room for growth or be relieved that a toxic employee is gone.

The best way to handle damage control will be through proper communication. It is unnecessary for you to control the narrative with a long explanation or debrief but inform the team with what is applicable. (More on this in the next chapter.)

You also need to deal with your own emotions surrounding someone's exit. Don't be consumed with emotions and ignore the employee during their transition period. If they are willing to give you two weeks' (or more) notice, use this time wisely. Discuss with the affected remaining employees to support them in gathering the needed knowledge to carry on without this exiting team member.

This is essential for the person who backs this role on the CT OAR Chart. Be sure they are ready to step in and that the handoff of any projects and/or clients is given adequate attention. You are still paying the exiting employee, and they should be working in exchange for that pay. You or someone on your team needs to be guiding them during this transition.

When Leaders Leave

Whether it's the owner of the company or someone in another leadership position, it's complicated and problematic when leaders leave. When a member of the Leadership Team exits, it should be handled with the utmost respect and care for the remaining team. Clarify to their subordinates who they will report to, even if temporarily.

It is a mistake to replace a Leadership Team member with an unqualified employee from within your company to simply fill the gap. Refer to *The Hiring Process* before posting the open position. While it's recommended to first post the job opening internally, it is unlikely that your company is loaded with leaders ready to make the move to your C-Suite. Remember that just as your company has a culture, your Leadership Team does as well. It's vital to keep the culture and trust in place, especially during the transition.

The debate on whether leadership can be taught is for another day. What should be clear is that you promote those qualified and experienced to leadership positions. This mistake can result in more people exiting, a lack of accountability, or micromanagement. All are detrimental to your culture and team.

Keep in mind that leaders have access to more information than the rest of your team. Be smart about how you remove access and create a successful Transition Plan, understanding that the exiting team member may no longer have the company's best interest in mind. While they may not intentionally cause harm, they are now invested in a future that doesn't include working for you. Even when parting on good terms, be sure to create a Transition Plan that includes healthy boundaries and oversight.

Owner Exit or Succession Plan

Succession planning is one of the most neglected aspects of owning a business. Yet, as a business owner, one responsibility you should prioritize is leadership succession. Maybe you're ready to retire, sell, or start a new business? Regardless of the reason for your exit, you want the company to continue. The goal of succession planning is to protect your business, family, employees, and clients. Whether it's a planned succession or an unfortunate tragedy, if your desire is that your company continues without you, this process should never be left to chance.

A solid succession can be planned and implemented over an extended period. This allows time for the original owner to work with the new leader or owner.

Ensuring that a business thrives when the leader leaves is incredibly **Succession should never be left to chance.**

difficult. Providing time for this transition will help protect what you've worked so hard to build.

To create a succession plan, first identify likely successors. Do you plan to sell the business or pass it along to a family member(s)? Will you offer to sell it to a key employee? Examine the key roles and responsibilities and document your desires, including time frames and so on.

If your desire is to sell, do you have assets and documented systems in place? We were once approached to purchase a business and had to break the news to the existing owner that they had nothing to sell. Be sure your company is scalable and saleable long before the time comes to sell it.

As you map out your plan, document everything and rely on input from the key professionals—lawyers and CPAs—you work with on other crucial business matters. They will play an important role in the proper implementation of your succession plan.

We've worked at the C-Suite level for small businesses that didn't have a succession plan in place. Trust us: it is not comforting to your Leadership Team to know that if something happens to you, their jobs, and the jobs of those they lead could be on the line. If you are truly building a valuable business, the time to protect it is now. Notify your key leadership that there is a plan in place and that their jobs are secure. This will reassure them that they are investing their time and talent into a company that will endure.

Unannounced Exits and Emergency Plans

After the desired succession plan has been established, create an additional plan for unexpected emergencies. Most likely, the original plan would take a considerable amount of time to implement. Now, look at it from the perspective of an emergency.

Who will temporarily take the reins while a long-term plan is implemented? Who will take on the owner's responsibilities? What is needed to support the current team and avoid disrupting services to your clients? While this can be included in your succession plan, a separate emergency plan that wouldn't be delayed by court proceedings or other legalities is necessary until the company can implement the more detailed, long-term plan.

Here are some more questions to consider: Who will oversee the transfer of ownership in your absence? Are you transferring ownership, and is the company to remain intact with the existing structure and team? Or will you transfer ownership and allow the new owner to implement changes they see fit? Can changes be made after a specific time frame? Think through what is best for you, your family, your team, and your clients. Then have your attorney draft a legally binding plan in the case of an emergency in which you are unable to act in your current role overseeing the company or any transition.

All of this further supports the requirement for CCCs, a strong OAR Chart, and—even better—a CT OAR Chart. Your emergency plan could be as simple as this:

"In the event of an emergency, in which I am unable to make decisions, or my untimely death, my Chief Operations Officer will take charge until my attorney has successfully implemented my succession plan on file."

Of course, you'll include the names of those key people and any appropriate financial compensation for the one taking temporary control of your company. This plan should be notarized and kept on file with your attorney and reviewed with those taking on any of the responsibilities. Discuss the plan in detail with your attorney to include all the legal requirements and any stipulations.

It's wise to have an emergency plan in place for the owner and any company leader's unexpected exit. Having a well-designed and implemented CT OAR Chart will assist with this as well. Who can step into the role temporarily, and what does that require? In the event of an untimely death or the permanent disability of any company leader, who will manage their role or specific department until a replacement can be brought in? If you only have one person in Accounting, who is cross-trained to manage payroll in their absence? Are they restricted on when they can vacation due to the timing of payroll? This is an unhealthy situation. In *The Retention Process,* we teach cross-training as a way to retain excellent team members. Utilizing the CT OAR Chart will guide your team in the absence of any team member, emergency or not.

Chapter Four

Communication and Collaboration

Few things are more important during a change event than communication from leaders who can paint a clear and confidence-inspiring vision of the future.

—Sarah Clayton

Just as each department should have an onboarding process in place, they should also have an exit process. When developing this process, all key players need to be involved. Collaborate with appropriate leaders or supervisors.

Use the Employee Exit Checklist to address all departments that may be involved when an employee leaves. These may look different or need adjustments, depending on the size of your company.

As previously mentioned, the entire exit process is typically owned by someone in the HR Department. If you are a small company without a dedicated HR Department, this may fall to someone in Finance, someone on your Leadership Team, or the direct supervisor of the exiting employee.

Employee Exit Checklist

HR
☐ Create and implement the Exit Communication Plan.

☐ Review and clarify with employee: contracts, insurance, and benefits enrollment.

☐ Request employee complete Exit ScoreCARD.

☐ Schedule and conduct Exit Interview.

☐ Update company records.

Department
☐ Collaborate with employee and other needed team members to create and implement the Transition Plan.

☐ Complete Role Survey.

☐ Request employee complete Leave a Legacy Worksheet (if applicable).

Payroll/Accounting
☐ Confirm final date for compensation, 401(k) contributions, or other applicable payroll deductions.

IT/Tech
☐ Collect company owned devices.

☐ Remove access or update passwords.

☐ Update website.

Admin Tasks
☐ Plan farewell event or appreciation gift.

☐ Update OAR Chart/CT OAR Chart.

☐ Update Team Directory.

☐ Remove birthday from team calendar.

Use our Exit Communication Plan included in the Toolbox to ensure the news of an employee's exit is communicated to those who need to know it, in the proper order, and correctly worded. Proper communication will benefit your remaining employees, the exiting employee, your clients, and your company culture.

Discuss the Exit Communication Plan with the exiting employee. The plan will include who you will tell and when, what the communication process will be, and what you intend to say.

Consider any particular team members who deserve or need to hear the news via a one-on-one conversation as opposed to a company-wide memo. If the employee followed the Team Handbook instructions and resigned to the HR Manager first, their direct supervisor would require a one-on-one

Proper communication benefits everyone.

conversation, as well as anyone who works closely with the exiting employee.

If communication isn't properly handled, others will come to their own conclusions about why someone is leaving. All communication should be initiated by the Leadership Team or HR Manager. All relevant team members must be included.

You cannot control how other employees will react to the information. Some may be shocked, concerned, or sad. Others may be happy or begin to wonder if they could be promoted to the newly vacated position.

You can control *what* is communicated and *how*. A team announcement within the hour following someone's resignation is not necessary but create a realistic timeline. This will vary depending on the role being vacated and the size of your company. Some departures may be a significant distraction. Start with those who need to know, as it applies to the work process, and then follow with the rest of the team.

Never ask an employee to "keep quiet" about a resignation or termination. Communicate your timeline with the exiting employee, as defined by the Exit Communication Plan, and ask that they respect this process.

Act quickly, as the exiting employee is typically eager for the announcement to be made and ready to say their **Create a realistic timeline.** goodbyes. Waiting fuels company gossip, and allowing the information to spread organically can be a detriment to your team dynamics. Prevent an inaccurate narrative from derailing your team. Misinformation or no information can leave your team feeling neglected and devalued and can create office drama.

Communicate to all departments when someone is leaving. Update all the necessary company information as previously mentioned. Keep the communication accurate and to the point. There is no reason to go into details as to why someone is leaving, as this information could be personal or private. In many cases, you may not truly understand their reason for leaving until they have completed the Exit ScoreCARD and Interview (we'll fully dive into these in a later chapter).

Example Email to Team:

Hello, team.

It is with great respect that we announce that Sydney Smith has resigned from her position as Customer Service Representative. Her team has been notified, and her position will temporarily be filled by Mark Lewis, as he is cross-trained for her role. A company announcement will come soon regarding the hiring specifics of the open job position. Sydney's last day will be June 9. We appreciate her dedication to the team over the last four years and wish her the best with her future endeavors.

Work to manage any morale issues that may arise as a result of the employee's exit. Ensure the remaining team members feel supported and valued. When communication is handled well, it creates stability for the rest of the company.

Assure your team that you will work to fill the position. This may mean new responsibilities for some team members. When possible, frame the conversation as an opportunity but only if you are sure the position will continue.

You should have clear SOPs and cross-training in place, as mentioned in Chapter 1. If not, as a leader, you must be willing to step into whatever capacity is appropriate until the position is filled. Once you are ready to post the position, you'll communicate again with your team. (More on assessing the position at the end of this chapter.)

Loose Ends

Until their final workday, the employee is still part of your team. Request all the needed items from them during their transition time—before they walk out the door for the last time—closing all the loops while you still have access to them and their knowledge of the role.

Provide a summarized list regarding any forthcoming compensation items. Include accrued vacation or PTO, if applicable, and details about transferring health or retirement benefits.

Anticipate questions they may have. What is the deadline for submitting their final expense report? Do they have any client deliverables outstanding? When and how will they receive their final paycheck? If a check is normally distributed at the place of business, will the final check be mailed? Or should they come pick it up?

In a termination situation, it may be best to mail the check. Asking an employee to come back to your place of business after you have fired them typically isn't a wise idea. It can be awkward, create tension, and in extreme situations, cause a scene. Even if the employee left on good terms, it may be a disruption if they come back. It's usually best to mail their final paycheck.

Perform a final review of any relevant contracts—nondisclosure, non-solicitation, or non-compete agreements. Clarify terms for the employee. Talk to them about any special clauses in these agreements and how they apply to their final days as an employee, as well as after their employment has ended. Contracts could include information about the intellectual property of the company or the consequences of exposing vital company data to competitors. Answer any lingering questions they may have.

As mentioned at the beginning of this chapter, update employee records. This will usually be handled by your HR or Finance Department. You need to have the exiting employee's most up-to-date phone number and mailing address on file, as you will have tax documents and a final paycheck to mail.

Assess the Position

As soon as the employee resigns and all appropriate announcements have been made, it is time to evaluate their position. Don't hesitate. Use your time wisely during the exiting employee's "notice." If you wait until they are gone and the hiring process takes longer than expected, you could be left with a gap for months. Examine the current Job Description and OAR Chart. (Revisit *The Hiring Process* for more on how to create an accurate job description and *The Onboarding Process* for how to create and utilize an OAR Chart). Does the description accurately capture the work being done? Or has the job evolved over the years? It may be time to write a new Job Description for this role. Reflect in order to look ahead.

Before posting the job opening and replacing the former employee, slow down long enough to assess their position in the company. Never assume that filling the role exactly as it was will be best for the company.

Spend time collaborating with the employee's direct supervisor. Discuss if now is the time to restructure this role or perhaps even the entire department. Has this role become

Reflect in order to look ahead.

obsolete? Use the Role Survey below to assess the role and the requirements for filling it.

Role Survey

How does this role support the Company Core Components?

List the **most important** tasks/processes this role completes on a regular basis.

List the tasks/processes **most frequently** completed by this role.

Are there any additional tasks that need to be completed by this role that currently aren't?

What skills or experience would strengthen this role?

Are there tasks this role does that would be more appropriate for a different role or department?

Is this role accountable to the correct leader and/or department?

In addition to the Role Survey, review the employee's previous quarterly and annual ScoreCARDs and Goal MAPs (see *The Retention Process*). View these through the lens of what the *ideal employee* would be for the position, instead of merely evaluating the employee who *was* filling the role. What needs to stay the same? Skills, experience, character, or personality? Identify gaps in training or talent.

After you've decided how you will move forward with the role responsibilities, engage the hiring team. Initiate your hiring process, including conducting a Capacity Check with your current team before posting the position (see *The Hiring Process for additional details*).

Communication throughout this process will be supported by the tools found in the Toolbox. If you haven't downloaded them yet, do so now and collaborate with your team on which tools you'll implement, who will own them, and train others on them.

At this point, you'll have two HR processes overlapping at the same time: the hiring process and a few things to wrap up with the exit process. There will be temporary discomfort or at a minimum an increased workload for some of your team. Be aware and plan accordingly. Keep communication a priority and work through this as a collaborative effort with your team.

Chapter Five

Transition Plan

Without a plan, even the most brilliant business can get lost. You need to have goals, create milestones, and have a strategy in place to set yourself up for success.

—Yogi Berra

As you created a carefully detailed plan for onboarding, the same needs to be made for an employee exit. The exiting team member needs to meet with their supervisor and HR representative to create their Transition Plan. Having a solid Transition Plan will keep productivity high and culture strong.

Remember, it is not your exiting employee's job to set the next employee up for success—that's your job. If they are on their way out the door, regardless of the reason, they are not as committed to your company as they were on their first day. It is naive to assign all the transition responsibilities to them.

Slow down and think through all the components of their job. The last situation you want to create is the need to reach out to a former employee for help because their transition was incomplete.

When Amanda left a previous employer, she gave a generous seven-week notice to help the company through a particularly busy season. She provided a few stipulations in her resignation, but the company had otherwise no written Transition Plan. As with many small business owners, this owner was disappointed that an integral part of his team was leaving. He let his emotions get the best of him and chose to avoid discussing the transition with Amanda.

Not only did the owner avoid working with Amanda to create a Transition Plan, but he also failed to hire her replacement or assign proper temporary support before her final day. He messaged Amanda three different times, regarding three different people (currently on the team) who would take over her role—none of whom were qualified, fully understood the role, nor had the capacity to take on additional responsibilities.

After seven weeks of little-to-no communication, she left the company with checklists and process documentation, but unfortunately, they didn't review any of it with her to understand how to train the replacement.

Not surprisingly, Amanda was contacted after her last day by remaining employees with questions about how to accomplish certain tasks. She was also contacted by vendors and contractors wondering when invoices would be paid.

Do not be like this business owner. Avoiding matters will not change them. Find out what you need to know while the employee is still on your team and create a Transition Plan so you can carry on after they're gone.

Your Transition Plan should include an outline of the changeover of roles and projects to support a smooth transition. See our template for creating a Transition Plan in the Toolbox.

At a minimum a Transition Plan should include the following:

Who—who will take over the role and duties temporarily (on the CT OAR Chart)

- Meet with the temporary replacement, their supervisor, and the exiting employee to bring everyone up-to-speed on projects, outstanding client deliverables, specific tasks, etc.

What—what job duties/projects the employee will continue to handle until exit date

When—duration of transition period and meetings to schedule, including:

- The exit interview on their final day
- A meeting with Tech to turn in assets
- Time for HR to review any contracts and compensation plans and to gather a forwarding address, etc.

Where—where important documentation, files, and other assets are located

How—how to accomplish goals, utilizing the Goal MAP (see Toolbox) during their transition time. Possible goals could include:

- creating a training video
- wrapping up a particular assignment
- handing off a project to another team member

Start with the immediate needs. It's a bit like triage. Who or what is critical and needs attention first? We will step through these urgent needs in the probable order of importance for your company:

1. Access and Assets—Company security is top priority.
2. Responsibilities—Avoid interruption of service or deliverables.
3. Knowledge—Learn what you can before they leave.

Access and Assets

It is unrealistic to rely on the integrity of the person leaving to protect your company. While we hope that they enjoyed working for your company and will be loyal to you and your clients on their way out the door, we know this is not the reality of many employee exits. You must take the necessary steps to protect your data, assets, and other proprietary information.

This is where proper setup is so important. Any documents in personal Google Drives and emails in personal inboxes, which cannot be accessed after an employee leaves, can spell disaster. Hopefully, your employee was onboarded well, and you have an Asset List that states the physical and digital assets they have access to. We discuss this list in *The Onboarding Process*. Each list is unique, depending on your company, the equipment you use, and the role of the employee.

Different departments might add to that list, but it will probably start with your Technology Department or possibly HR.

There are three components to this list:

1. Physical technological assets/ equipment, such as laptops, phones, and tablets
2. Other physical company assets/ equipment, such as company vehicles, operating equipment, security badges, credit cards, etc.
3. Digital assets, such as software programs and accounts with unique log-in information

If such a list exists, verify that all physical assets have been turned in and that all digital assets have had their access revoked or log-in credentials updated. If the list doesn't exist, create it for the exiting employee first to utilize in this process but then create one for everyone in your company for adequate security moving forward.

For their company email accounts, passwords must be changed. Also, their email inbox should be monitored or forwarded to someone else in the company. This information should be documented in the Transition Plan.

Don't leave your company at risk of security issues. When assets are unprotected or unmonitored, your former employee might wipe their computer of all the company documents they no longer need without realizing they were the sole owner of those documents, and now no one in the company can access them.

If you have one login for an account shared by many, it will need to be changed when one of those "many" exits the company. If at all possible, avoid such practices for this and other security reasons, and assign each individual a unique user name and password so that you can identify who is in the account or making changes at any given time.

We've seen it all in regard to account security. Emails not forwarded—the simplest of tasks overlooked—will leave clients and vendors wondering if you're still in business. Passwords not updated, document ownership not changed, client information exposed to too many employees and then not protected upon employee exits ... these mistakes create chaos. If you haven't taken a close look at how your company shares critical information, discuss this task at your next leadership meeting, and decide who will take ownership of creating order in this area of your organization.

Responsibilities

What are the responsibilities of this role? Who will handle them moving forward?

Having your people cross-trained ahead of someone's exit is vital. Are there any tasks or responsibilities that need to be added to the role—something the exiting employee started doing that wasn't in their original Job Description or on the OAR Chart?

Prioritize daily tasks and weekly responsibilities of the role. Does this role send weekly reports to the team? Who then will take this on? Are they responsible for updating the metrics before a meeting? Delegate all their tasks. Be sure to think through tasks that are occasionally performed as well, such as quarterly reports or semiannual budget updates.

Clearly define when a task/project is handed off and who is responsible for it. This is imperative when an employee has given a two-week notice (or longer).

Will one person take on everything? Or will the work be redistributed among several team members? Is any training required before others can capably complete the job duties?

All responsibilities must be reassigned to another employee—even if it's temporary. Never leave certain tasks unassigned while waiting to hire a replacement. All processes and tasks must be owned by someone before the end of the notice period if one was given.

Be sure to discuss project status updates with the exiting employee and the employee filling in. Are they currently participating in any team collaborations and with whom?

Don't neglect clients or projects during the transition time. Workflow should continue without disruption. Aim for no interruption of services or production. Maintain quality control.

If the exiting employee deals directly with clients, facilitate a handoff meeting or email. You want to avoid the awkward and possibly alarming conversation with a client, "Oh, Joe? He doesn't work here anymore." Same for vendors or other specific contacts outside of your organization—practice clear communication.

Example Handoff Emails:

Hi, [Client Name].

I'd like to introduce you to Mary Smith in our office. I've moved to a part-time role as a Client Services Associate, and Mary has become our new Administrative Assistant. Since I will no longer be in the office every day, I want to connect the two of you so that if you have any questions or need any assistance, you can be sure to get a quick answer from your new point of contact, Mary.

Please let us know if you have any questions or need anything before your meeting. We are happy to help!

Hi, [Vendor Name].

I'd like to introduce you to Mary Smith in our office. I'm moving out of my role as Client Services Associate, and Mary will be taking my place. I want to connect the two of you so that if you have any questions or need any assistance, you can be sure to get a quick response and know your point of contact moving forward.

*Please let us know if you have any
questions or need anything.*

If possible, ask the exiting employee to document important processes or create a training video. These should include details of day-to-day responsibilities. Ideally, this is documented as an SOP well before an employee resigns or transfers and is used for cross-training and process improvement. Waiting until someone gives their notice to ask them to document their roles and responsibilities may be one of the reasons they are leaving. If you don't value their position enough to work on ways to improve their work experience, they probably won't feel valued either. Now that they have one foot out the door, they aren't going to give their best effort to support a team that didn't support them.

If you have neglected to document processes or some of those processes have changed, ask the exiting employee to walk through their day-to-day responsibilities with their temporary replacement (the person who backs up their role on the CT OAR Chart) and capture the information as they go. This will give you two sets of eyes on the process and allow for clarifying questions. Confirm they understand how to document the details, including necessary links, logins, deadlines, and so on.

Now, if you haven't found backups for each position in your company, cross-trained those backups, and documented the tasks they would be backing up, it's time. Have your team identify within each role what processes need to be documented, and work with their backups (on the CT OAR Chart) to ensure they have what they need to fill in for one another at any given time. Present this as an opportunity for them to discover areas for improvement, and point out that by having everyone cross-trained, there will be more flexibility in vacation scheduling and time off.

Knowledge

Transferring knowledge is much more difficult than transferring assets or responsibilities. There is no simple export or download function for this information.

Depending on the position and how long the employee has been with the company, their knowledge may be minimal or significant. Their knowledge can be especially critical if their job revolves around numerous relationships. Information about specific clients' and vendors' personalities, for instance, isn't usually documented, but it is knowledge that would be beneficial to the role replacement.

Schedule meetings with the supervisor, applicable team members, leadership, or even the incoming employee to review some of their projects and relationships, revealing any knowledge gaps between the documentation and the reality of the role. When working through an employee's Transition Plan, supervision is a must. This doesn't mean micromanaging, but supervisors and leadership need to keep a close eye to ensure work is completed well and undocumented knowledge is captured to pass on. Utilize job shadowing when possible during an employee's transition time.

The goal is that before the employee walks out the door, or logs off on that last day, you have all the knowledge necessary to successfully manage their job duties. Use the Leave a Legacy Worksheet found in the Toolbox to capture previously undocumented ideas and information that the exiting employee may desire to leave behind. This worksheet is best used by someone who has been in the role for a long time and cares about the legacy they leave within the company. It could also be useful for someone who was dissatisfied with company procedures, as they may leave ideas for better methods not previously shared.

Every employee deserves to feel worthy in the workplace—from their hiring through their last day with the company. Having a solid Transition Plan in place along with your CT OAR Chart will set you in the right direction.

Chapter Six

Examine the Why

*The greatest danger in times
of turbulence is not the turbulence
—it is to act with yesterday's logic.*

—Peter Drucker

As you go through an employee exit, you tend to focus more on how you will overcome the situation and who will own the role next. However, it is imperative that you intentionally take time to also find out the "why." Why is this employee really leaving? This requires digging deeper and goes beyond simply asking "Why?"

when they turn in a resignation. Create a system to collect authentic feedback from all exiting employees. This feedback may add tremendous value to your company.

All businesses should be aware of ways they can improve. We provide two tools you can use to gather information from your exiting employee.

1. The Exit ScoreCARD
2. Exit Interview Sample Questions

Both tools give the exiting employee a chance to be heard and to assist you in assessing their role. Reassure confidentiality to the employee completing the ScoreCARD or interview. The goal is honest feedback. They will be more open if they are confident in knowing who will or won't see their responses.

Exit ScoreCARD

The Exit ScoreCARD will give you more quantitative data. Utilize the ranking scale but also provide a place for open feedback. This provides the exiting employee the opportunity to write comments that they might not have been brave enough to share face-to-face.

Have the exiting employee complete the Exit ScoreCARD prior to meeting with HR for the Exit Interview. If you have any follow-up questions, the Exit Interview would be the proper time to ask them. Again, this is not a time for blame or defensiveness, but if you need specific examples that support their ScoreCARD comments, ask direct questions.

Share the ScoreCARD feedback only with those who can improve the situation or circumstance. This is not the time to share the results across the company. Honor the confidentiality you assured the exiting employee. Any negative comments, scores, or suggestions should be reviewed by HR and the former employee's supervisor to discuss a healthy plan of action to improve the situation. Once solutions have been discussed, the information can be taken to a Leadership Team meeting, if necessary, to close the loop or notify other departments of any changes to improve the situation.

Here is a sample of a completed ScoreCARD.

Exit ScoreCARD

Employee Name Brad Robbins   **Final Date** 8/26/22

Rate on a 1–10 scale (in the box provided).
Provide a specific example (positive or negative) for each.

9 **C**ulture –How healthy do you feel the workplace culture is? Were the Core Values evident in the day-to-day operations of the company?

This company has a great culture. Welcoming, amazing teamwork. Leadership always willing to step in and help.

8 **A**bility–Did your department and/or supervisor provide you with the feedback and tools to do your job to the best of your ability?

Yes, from tool training to one-on-one support, I had everything I needed to perform my tasks.

7 **R**ole–Did you see how your role supported the company's bigger Vision and Mission? Did you feel you could openly communicate with your supervisor and that information was clearly communicated throughout the company?

Communication overall was good. A couple of items would slip through the cracks regarding company-wide announcements at times. These affected how I performed my role.

10 **D**esire–Was there a desire for growth in your department or role recognized by leadership?

Yes, Carol supported my growth tremendously throughout my time here. She was supportive and encouraging with my professional development.

Provide 2–3 brief phrases that describe your experience both positive and negative in your role.

Professional growth & development.

Amazing collabortoin on my team

Would you recommend our company to a customer? (please provide a short explanation)

Absolutely. Quality products with fantastic customer support.

Would you recommend our company to a friend as a place of employment? (please provide a short explanation)

Yes, the environment is supportive and encourages growth

Other notes or concerns we need to be aware of

This place will be missed!

Exit Interview

An Exit Interview should be conducted within the last few days, up to a week prior to the employee's exit. But don't wait until the last day in case you need them to take additional action on items discussed during the interview.

Be sure to document the interview. This is best handled by your HR Department or representative. At the very least, the employee's direct supervisor should not conduct the interview. This will allow the employee the chance to speak freely (as they may not be inclined to when speaking to their direct supervisor) and allows HR to compile information, notice trends in ScoreCARDs and Exit Interviews, and address any possible concerns with the relevant team members or departments.

Ask tough questions. But be prepared for responses that may be equally tough to hear. The questions you ask during this interview should encourage honest, in-depth responses from the employee. Go into this interview with an open mind, regardless of the circumstances surrounding the employee's departure.

Structure questions in a way that will initiate open dialogue without fear. Use open-ended questions instead of yes-or-no questions. Ask follow-up questions for clarification. Request that the employee expands on their thoughts or statements, if applicable. Dig as deep as the employee is willing to go to provide you with a complete picture of the required improvements. Providing this opportunity may help a disgruntled employee to vent about issues, instead of sharing publicly on social media or other outlets.

When an employee is on their way out the door, they will likely be transparent, as they perceive they have nothing left at stake. Depending on the relationship and how the employee is leaving, their feedback could be harsh. Now is not the time to debate. Simply gather. Seek clarification but avoid defensiveness and blame. Remember the intention and reiterate that to the employee. This interview is meant to gather feedback that can be used to identify improvements to better serve your team and clients, not to make excuses.

Ask about multiple areas of the business:

1. Communication
2. Employee recognition
3. Culture
4. Exit/offboarding process
5. Client perception

Feedback on what needs improvement is obviously valuable. Focus on the positive as well. This can help your company know what is working—what systems or programs are worth continuing. Finishing the interview on a positive note will also leave the employee feeling valued and with a positive last impression.

An Exit Interview shouldn't be forced. You may have employees who wish not to participate, and that's okay. Hopefully, they will at minimum complete the Exit ScoreCARD.

Offer a recommendation if the employee is leaving on good terms. Remember that if the employee stays in the same industry, you might see them again.

Here are suggested Exit Interview questions:

Exit Interview Questions

If you could change anything about the organization, what would you choose?

Did you voice your concerns to anyone else at the company? If yes, who and how were they received?

What are the biggest risks you see for our company?

Why did you begin looking for another job?

How did your day-to-day tasks compare to your expectations when hired?

Describe the style of management you worked under. What did you think of the way you were managed?

What is your opinion of how communication is handled across the company?

Do you feel that employee recognition programs are sufficient? What would you change?

What benefits or programs did you feel were missing from the organization?

What did you appreciate most about working here?

From your perspective, what is the average client perception of our company?

What do you hear others saying both internally and externally about our company?

What would make this a better place to work?

Do you have any comments or suggestions on how to improve our exit process?

Take Action

Feedback given during an exit will provide invaluable opportunities for you to improve your company and employee experience, boosting employee retention. Don't get stuck in a cycle of turnover.

Take the feedback you receive and examine any pain points shared by the exiting employee.

Feedback provides opportunity.

What could have been handled differently? What actions may boost future employee retention? Was the employee overworked? Did they feel burned out or underappreciated? Underpaid? Was there a toxic culture? Lack of career development? Unfulfilled promises? Lack of boundaries? Maybe the Job Description they were hired for didn't meet the role or expectations placed on them once hired?

Not all feedback will require action. There will be isolated incidents or issues. But keep an eye out for patterns. An essential skill of an emotionally intelligent leader or one working in an HR role is being observant enough to notice patterns and identify the root source of issues.

Identifying root issues might require a hard and uncomfortable look in the mirror. Why is someone really leaving? Are you the problem? Is your culture the issue? Pay attention to the elephant in the room. If one person is leaving your company due to a specific pain point, it is probable that you have a remaining employee who is also frustrated by the same issue. Unless you address this pain point, it's only a matter of time before the remaining employee exits too.

If the feedback requires actions to be taken across the company, brainstorm the issue with the supervisor and take ideas to your

Leadership Team. Continuing a collaborative effort with open communication during this part of the exit process is necessary.

Avoiding Turnover

If the employee's supervisor was truly caught off guard by their resignation, it's time to take stock of how your leadership connects with their teams. A leader who is in tune with their team will never be shocked by a resignation.

Refer to the previous books in *The Team Solution Series*. Communication is the overarching theme. Open and healthy communication will keep your leaders in the know regarding employee issues and satisfaction. Utilizing the tools in each of the books will help you hire better, onboard smarter, and create a culture of worth in the workplace, resulting in minimal turnover.

Remember the bottom line for employees: they want to operate in their grace-given talents while being respected, recognized, and compensated accordingly. On the surface, this seems simple, but the reality is that it requires effort.

If turnover continues to be an issue in any particular department, you need to examine the leadership and culture within that department. Also, examine outside departments that may influence the patterns you see there. For example, if you have a department with clear processes and procedures but high turnover rates, identify the root cause. Perhaps it's the behavior of leaders outside the department, who are unwilling to follow procedure and continually disrupt the workflow. The department director can only prevent turnover to an extent if the leadership above continues to wreak havoc in their department's workflow. This is why accountability at every level of your organization is vital.

Examining why an employee leaves can be difficult. Simply being aware of the issue is not enough. Confront the problem and work through the challenge. The effort put into these actions will benefit the entire company. A healthy company is one who works to continually improve.

Chapter Seven

Wrap-up and Resources

*Leadership is never an avenue
to be self-serving but a platform
to render great service to people.*

—Ifeanyi Enoch Onuoha

Regardless of why your employee is exiting, help them leave on a positive note. Thank them for the work they have done for your company and wish them well. If appropriate, write a thank-you note, buy a gift, or throw a farewell party (especially if it is a retirement).

As you work through the exit process, remember your Core Values. Your current employees and potential future employees will see how you handle an employee exit. Don't let your mishandling of one exit be the reason another employee decides to call it quits. If there is overlap between the exit of one employee and the onboarding of another, the new hire may also be watching. Show respect to the employee who is leaving. Never bad-mouth them or broadcast their flaws to their replacement. Your actions should show that people are more valuable than your bottom line.

When someone leaves, they will either be a supporter of your company or an adversary. Reputation and brand can be affected by your handling of an employee exit. Former employees are your best (or worst) forms of advertising. Making an employee's departure a positive experience will affect how they talk about your company to family, friends, and colleagues, some of whom may consider applying to work for you or becoming a client. Keep in mind that ex-employees can be excellent marketing and ambassadors for your company. Or they can be the reason someone doesn't want to conduct business with you. Preserve the networking opportunities you may have with this former employee.

If the employee was a valuable asset to your company and enjoyed working with you, they could be a boomerang employee. Leave the door open if you're willing to work with them again in the future. Some exits may be circumstantial, and when the situation changes, the employee might treasure the opportunity to work with you again. If you feel the same way, and if it's the right fit for the team, welcome them back. We encourage you to go through the hiring process with them again to be certain they fit the role and it's not just because you like them. Be smart and don't hire out of loyalty or friendship if the company doesn't have an open spot for them. They may be the right person, but if the seat is not right for them, it's not the right move.

That's a Wrap!

As with each book in *The Team Solution Series*, we've provided a free Toolbox available for download at thejoyofpursuit.com/exit. We encourage you to walk through these tools with your HR representatives as well as your Leadership Team. We understand that each of the four processes shared in this series has many moving parts. That is why we broke each process down into easily digestible books with corresponding tools. Some tools overlap and can be used across your organization for different purposes.

We know there are many ways to tackle these processes; you may already have systems in place. Our hope is that one tool or piece of advice can be incorporated into what you are already doing to improve your workplace culture and increase success.

If you are building your business from the ground up, congratulations on getting an early start on the solutions set forth in this series. Creating an organization of accountability and respect and setting yourself up to grow a team of dedicated, valued employees will pay dividends in the long run. If you've been in business for any length of time, implementing these processes now shows your team that you appreciate them and that you want to build a solid business with an unshakeable foundation. This will only increase their loyalty to and sense of security within your company.

Identifying gaps in existing businesses can be difficult when you are running the daily operations. If you recognize the strain but can't pinpoint the issue, we encourage you to reach out. We can evaluate your current model and recognize where improvements need to be made. If your business is sizable, you may want your team to read this series and self-implement the processes. With the right people in the right seats, this can be accomplished, and your company will reap the benefits. If you are a smaller team, or you have unfilled roles in your HR Department, having a professional assist with teaching the tools, aligning your Company Core Components, and providing clear processes will expedite your results.

And, of course, leaving us a review on Amazon (regardless of where you purchased the book) will help other businesses find the processes that are now helping your company. We personally read each review and appreciate your taking the time to provide feedback.

Here's to joy in all your pursuits!

Download The Exit Process Toolbox at
TheJoyOfPursuit.com/Exit

- Department Transfer Checklist
- Employee Exit Checklist
- Role Survey
- Exit ScoreCARD
- Exit Interview Questions
- Leave a Legacy Worksheet
- Transition Plan Template
- Exit Communication Plan
- Goal MAP
- Team Capacity Check

Acknowledgments

As we wrap up this series, our hearts are full, and we stand amazed at how God is using these books to make an impact in workplaces globally. We want to thank each and every one of you who have taken the time to invest in your teams by reading and implementing the words we've poured out.

Exits are never easy. We'd like to acknowledge those we've left behind when we've moved on. Our hope is that we made a difference and left a legacy through our grace-given gifts. We are humbled that through this series, our workshops, and consulting, our unique gifts are multiplied reaching businesses of all sizes around the world.

From the depths of our hearts, we thank you for purchasing the books in this series. We are thrilled with the #1 New Release success and are fueled to continue to share our unique processes in our next several series. Whether you are a family member, friend, colleague, or business builder, we appreciate every review, mention, recommendation, and opportunity to share the processes God has made clear to us so that we can serve others.

Amanda is known both personally and professionally for her consistency, clarity, and commitment. Her grace-given gifts of practicality and focus allow her to keep an accurate perspective in life and business. She is level-headed and gives attention to the necessary priorities without distractions slowing her down. Amanda is an action-taker with a well-thought-out plan of attack in hand.

Throughout her work history, Amanda has frequently been known as the most dependable team member. She began her career with numbers and finances but grew to discover a passion for the people-side of business in Human Resources. She has a talent for identifying uniqueness in others, encouraging them to know their worth and abilities, all while gracefully holding them accountable for their actions.

Despite years of working for a publishing company, Amanda never thought she would be an author. She is now a four-time published author with an entire series for small businesses. *The Team Solution Series: HR Coaching to Grow Teams and Profit* provides more than ideas—the books are full implementation plans to guide you and your team through the employee journey. The content blends Amanda's unparalleled organizational skills with her knowledge of HR practices. Her exceptional ability to improve efficiency and processes in organizations will serve countless small business owners and strengthen their teams.

Throughout the writing and publishing process of *The Team Solution Series* (and thanks to being business partners with a top-notch book coach), Amanda knows that if she can write a book, anyone can. Together with her business partner, Brenda Haire, they created the Author Business Network, providing authors with the tools needed to successfully write, publish, market, and build a business around their books.

Amanda and her two children live at the foothills of the Smoky Mountains in Tennessee. She enjoys hiking with her kids, cooking, and gardening, especially cultivating flowers. She's known for having some of the most beautiful blooms in town. One of the greatest joys of her life is watching her children grow and guiding them to pursue their passions.

Connect with Amanda
LinkedIn.com/in/AmandaJPainter

Brenda's had over forty jobs and has been working since she was twelve. She's never been fired and is not ashamed of her work history. Brenda always worked her way up, out, and on to the next adventure. Many see this as risky and call her fearless. She would tell you that fear was always a factor—she just chose faith instead.

After being told she was a nobody by a publisher, Brenda struggled with her identity as a writer. Not one to give up, she pursued her dream and released her first book, *Save the Butter Tubs!: Discover Your Worth in a Disposable World*, in 2018.

Brenda was immediately hired by her publishing agency after her book was released, and she went on to become the president of the company. An entrepreneur at heart, once again she left on top and now uses her experience to serve individuals and small businesses around the world as the CEO and cofounder of Joy of Pursuit. Brenda created the Author Business Network with her business partner,

Amanda Painter, and together they help authors build businesses around their books.

As a speaker, Brenda shares keynotes and workshops that transform audiences. Whether she is speaking about purpose, publishing, or small business, her deepest desire is to help you shine your light by operating in your grace-given gifts. She considers herself a moved soul—so moved by her encounters with God that she can't help but move in response. She wants the same for you—to encounter God in a way that you can't help but live a life worthy of your calling.

She and her hubs (as she lovingly refers to him on social media), Darren, are both military veterans. They enjoy hiking and chasing waterfalls across the United States and live in Texas with their beautifully blended and expanding family.

Connect with Brenda
Facebook.com/BrendaHaire
Instagram.com/BrendaAHaire
LinkedIn.com/in/Brenda Haire

Empower Your Team
Elevate Your Business

» Strategies to Find and Keep Top Talent.

» Techniques that Boost Employee Engagement and Reduce Turnover.

» Tools to Ensure Smooth Transitions and Protect Your Business.

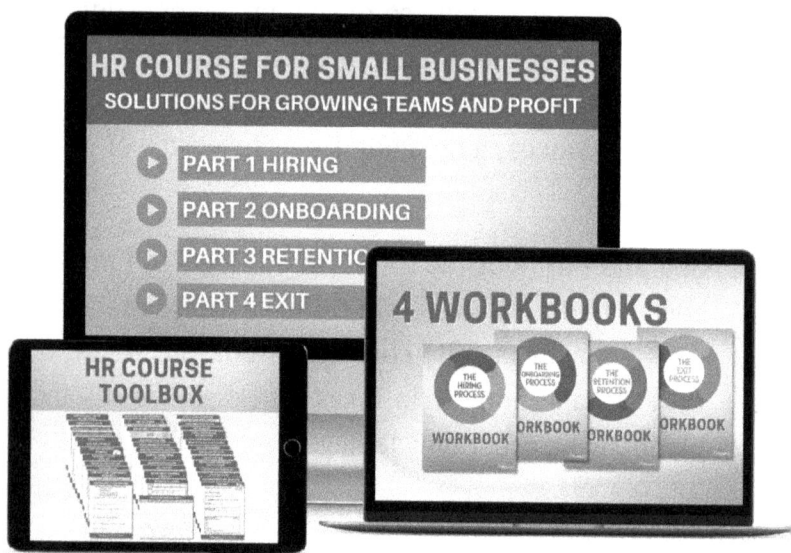

HR COURSE FOR SMALL BUSINESSES
SOLUTIONS FOR GROWING TEAMS AND PROFIT

▶ PART 1 HIRING

▶ PART 2 ONBOARDING

▶ PART 3 RETENTIO

▶ PART 4 EXIT

4 WORKBOOKS

THE HIRING PROCESS WORKBOOK

THE ONBOARDING PROCESS WORKBOOK

THE RETENTION PROCESS WORKBOOK

THE EXIT PROCESS WORKBOOK

HR COURSE TOOLBOX

Unlock the Full Potential
of Your Team »ENROLL NOW

TheJoyofPursuit.com/HR-Course

Revolutionize Your Business
with Our HR Consulting Services

Executive Consultant

Amanda J. Painter

Tailored Solutions for Your HR Challenges

》 Streamline Processes

》 Boost Productivity

》 Reduce Costs

Start Today!
TheJoyOfPursuit.com/
store/p/HRconsult

Receive Exclusive HR Insights, Industry News, and Best Practices Straight to Your Inbox.

CUT >>
THE >>
CHAOS

One email per month to take you and your business from tired and busy to thriving and productive!

Try it today

Tools.TheJoyOfPursuit.com/CutTheChaos

Take the next step in creating a culture of growth and fulfillment of purpose.

COMPLETE THE
TEAM SOLUTION SERIES

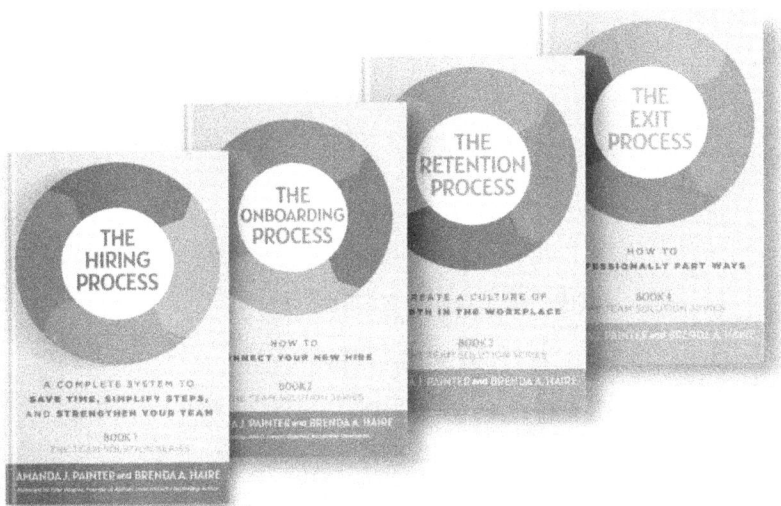

TheJoyOfPursuit.com/Books

Transform Your Workplace

Build a Custom Workshop for Your Team

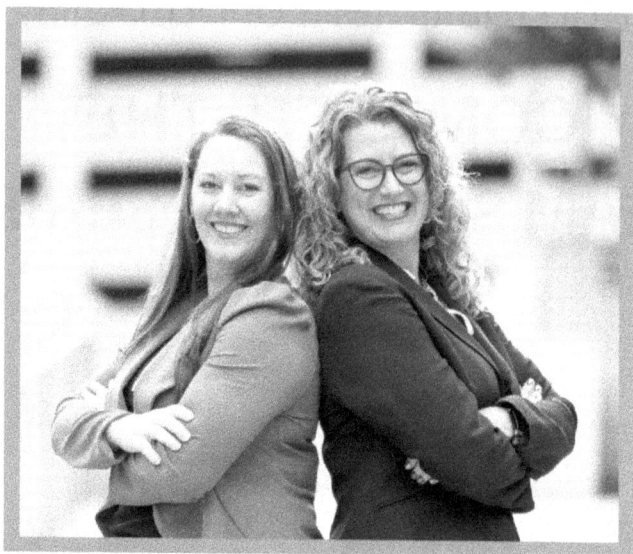

Higher Productivity
Efficient Meetings
Lower Turnover
Engaged Employees
Cohesive Leadership Team

It's Time to Create a
Joyful Workplace
for YOU and Your Team!

TheJoyOfPursuit.com/Workshops

Buy in Bulk

for Your Human Resource Team,
Directors, or Leadership Team

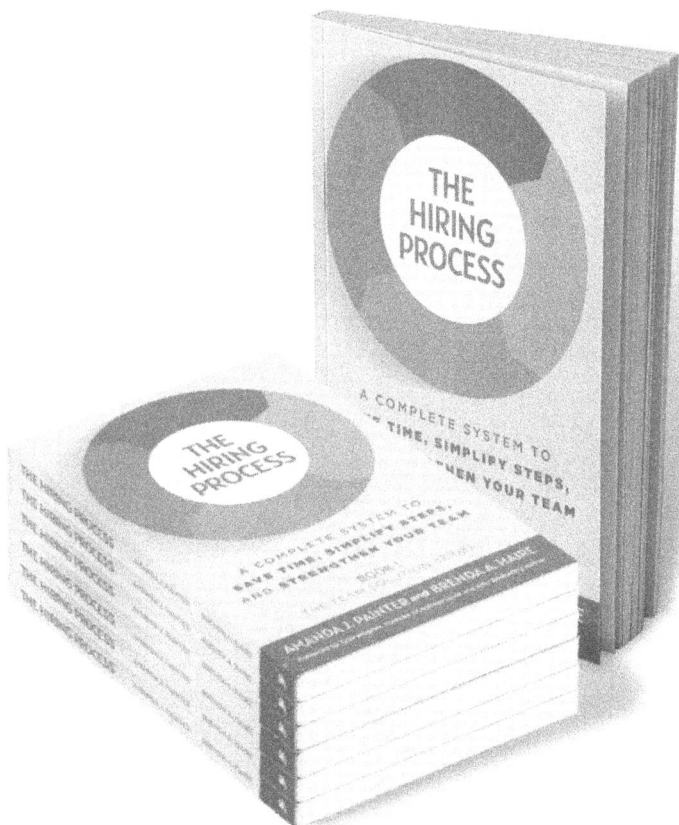

TheJoyofPursuit.com/Books

www.ingramcontent.com/pod-product-compliance
Lightning Source LLC
Chambersburg PA
CBHW071420210326
41597CB00020B/3590